The Art and Techniques of Simulation

The Art and Techniques of Simulation was prepared under the auspices of the American Statistical Association—National Council of Teachers of Mathematics Joint Committee on the Curriculum in Statistics and Probability.

This book is part of the Quantitative Literacy Project, which was funded in part by the National Science Foundation.

The Art and Techniques of Simulation

Mrudulla Gnanadesikan
Fairleigh Dickinson University

Richard L. Scheaffer
University of Florida

Jim Swift
Nanaimo School District
Nanaimo, British Columbia, Canada

DALE SEYMOUR PUBLICATIONS

Cover: John Edeen and Francesca Angelesco
Technical Art: Colleen Donovan
Cartoonist: Barry Geller
Editing and Production: Larry Olsen

Printed in the United States of America. Published simultaneously in
Canada.

This publication was prepared as part of the American Statistical
Association Project—Quantitative Literacy—with partial support of the
National Science Foundation Grant No. DPE-8317656. Any opinions,
findings, conclusions, or recommendations expressed in this publication
are those of the authors and do not necessarily represent the views of the
National Science Foundation. These materials shall be subject to a
royalty-free, irrevocable, worldwide, nonexclusive license in the United
States Government to reproduce, perform, translate, and otherwise use
and to authorize others to use such materials for Government purposes.

ISBN 0-86651-336-1

Order Number DS01704

c d e f g h i j —MA— 9 5 4 3 2 1 0

DALE
SEYMOUR
PUBLICATIONS
P.O. BOX 10888
PALO ALTO, CA 94303

CONTENTS

PREFACE

This is the third in a series of publications produced by the ASA-NCTM Joint Committee on the Curriculum in Statistics and Probability. The others are *Exploring Data, Exploring Probability,* and *Exploring Surveys and Information from Samples.* These four units cover the basic concepts of statistics and probability. The approach emphasizes use of real data, active experiments, and student participation. There are no complicated formulas or abstract mathematical concepts to confuse or mislead you.

The Art and Techniques of Simulation builds on the material in *Exploring Probability* and shows how practical problems, from the simple to the complex, can be solved, at least approximately, by using simple simulations. Many of the Applications herein are readily adapted to the computer, but all can be done without access to a computer.

———————

I. INTRODUCTION

Simulation is a procedure developed for answering questions about real problems by running experiments that closely resemble the real situation. Many of you may have worked through the unit on probability and done experiments to estimate probabilities. You have also found probabilities by collecting data and observing the values of the variables. This unit will build on the experience you got from the previous units dealing with both probability and exploring data. It will show you how to find probabilities for complex events and how to understand the behavior and estimate the outcomes of real processes.

Suppose we want to find the probability that a three-child family contains exactly one girl. We can find a theoretical answer for this probability if we know something about the rules of probability. We could also estimate this probability if we could observe a large number of three-child families and count the number that contain exactly one girl. But what if we cannot compute the theoretical answer and do not have the time to locate three-child families for observation? The best plan, in this case, might be to *simulate* the outcomes for three-child families.

One way to accomplish this for our example is to toss coins to represent the three births. A head could represent the birth of a girl. Then, observing exactly one head in a toss of three coins would be similar, in terms of probability, to observing exactly one girl in a three-child family. We could easily toss the three coins many times to estimate the probability of seeing exactly one head. The result gives us an estimate of the probability of seeing exactly one girl in a three-child family. This is a simple problem to simulate, but the idea is very useful in complex problems for which theoretical probabilities may be nearly impossible to obtain.

Simulation is a technique that evolved as people tried to find ways to answer questions about the behavior of complex processes under varying conditions. For instance, in the process of designing the electronic guidance systems of a space shuttle, scientists would be interested in the probability of system failure for various possible designs. One way of estimating this probability would be actually to build the systems and test them in real flight conditions, but this would be very time consuming and expensive. Another way of estimating this probability is to simulate the performance of the guidance systems on a computer. The systems can then be observed through many simulated tests quite quickly, and the probabilities of failure can be estimated quite well. The simulations allow the scientist to choose the design that has the smallest probability of failure.

Simulations can also be used to help determine the outcomes of business ventures. Suppose you wanted to set up a lemonade stand but wanted to do so only if it were profitable. You could experiment with different prices per glass of lemonade and different lemonade mixtures while conducting your business, but you might use up your whole summer before you settled on the best price and best mixture. A better way to proceed would be to collect some data on important variables and simulate the performance of your lemonade stand. For example, you could ask some of your friends if they would pay 30 cents per glass as opposed to 20 cents per glass. You could also let them taste two different mixtures to see which one they preferred. The chance of selling a glass of lemonade might be affected by the weather, so you might want to estimate the proportion of sunny days in the summer for your location. This information could then be used to simulate the performance of your lemonade business. The simulation could allow you to estimate, for example, your chances of selling a glass of mixture A for 30 cents on a sunny day. You could also estimate your expected profits for a month.

This unit will provide an introduction to simulation techniques. It will begin with simple models for obtaining an estimate of the probability of an event and then progress toward answering more complex questions, such as "How much money can I expect to make from my lemonade stand?" The approach will *not* be computer dependent, although computer programs make the actual simulations somewhat easier to perform.

II. A SIMULATION MODEL

We will now look at one simulation problem in great detail. We will set up an eight-step process that will carry us through this problem. The same eight-step process should be used in all the Applications in this book.

Step 1 State the problem clearly.

It is important that the problem be stated so that all necessary information is given and the objective of the simulation is clear.

Example: Mary has not studied for her history exam. She knows none of the answers on a seven-question true–false exam, and she decides to guess at all seven. Estimate the probability that Mary will guess the correct answers to four or more of the seven questions.

Step 2 Define the key components.

The outcomes of most real situations we study will be made up of a series of key components. It is important to define these components clearly since they form the basis of our simulation.

Example: Answering the seven questions on Mary's exam forms the seven key components in this case. We must first simulate the answering of one question and then repeat that simulation six more times for the remaining questions.

Step 3 State the underlying assumptions.

Most real problems require some simplifying assumptions before a solution can be found. These assumptions should be clearly stated.

Example: We assume that Mary's guessing makes her equally likely to answer true or false on each question. Thus, Mary has a probability of one half of guessing the correct answer to any one question. We also assume that her guesses are independent—that is, her answer to any one question is not affected by her answers to previous questions.

Step 4 Select a model to generate the outcomes for a key component.

We model a key component by choosing a simple device to generate chance outcomes with probabilities to match those of the real situation.

Example: Since the probability that Mary guesses the correct answer on any one question is one half, we can model her answering a single question by tossing a coin and letting a head (H) stand for "correct answer" and a tail (T) stand for "incorrect answer."

Step 5 Define and conduct a trial.

A trial consists of a series of key component simulations that stops when the situation of interest has been simulated once.

Example: Mary is to guess seven answers in a row. Therefore, tossing a fair coin seven times simulates her answering one complete exam.

Step 6   Record the observation of interest.

Recall the objective of the simulation from step 1. Now, record the information necessary to reach that objective. In most cases, we will record whether the trial was favorable to an event of interest. In some cases, other numerical outcomes will be noted.

Example: After the coin is tossed seven times, we observe the number of heads. If the number of heads is four or more, then the trial is favorable to the event "Mary answers four or more questions correctly." We usually want to keep a record of the outcome for each trial.

Step 7   Repeat steps 5 and 6 a large number of times (at least 50).

The accurate estimation of a probability requires the experiment to contain many trials. If the experiment is done by hand, then 50 trials may be enough. If the experiment is done by computer, then 1,000 or more trials can be run. (When conducting the experiments by hand, divide the work so that no one student does more than about five trials.)

Example: Toss the coin seven more times and record the number of heads. Repeat this process for 50 trials of seven coin tosses.

Step 8   Summarize the information and draw conclusions.

We can now estimate the probability of an event of interest, *E*, by looking at

$$\frac{\text{the number of trials favorable to } E}{\text{the total number of trials in the experiment}}$$

Other summary statistics can be calculated. For example, we might be interested in the average value of some numerical outcomes.

Example: We can now estimate the probability that Mary correctly answers four or more questions by looking at

$$\frac{\text{the number of trials containing four or more heads}}{\text{the total number of trials in the experiment}}$$

We can also calculate the average number of correct answers per trial and use this as an estimate of the expected number of correct answers when guessing on a seven-question true–false exam.

Table 1 shows the results of a computer simulation of the true–false exam, with 100 trials. Table 1 was obtained by using a computer program written for Apple II computers. A listing of this program is shown on page 5. Your instructor can supply you with computer programs to work all of the Application problems in this book.

SIMPRO1

Program to Simulate Trials with Repeated Coin Tosses

```
10    PRINT "PROGRAM TO SIMULATE TRIALS WITH REPEATED"
20    PRINT "COIN TOSSES IN EACH TRIAL"
30    PRINT
40    PRINT "YOU WILL HAVE TO ENTER THE NUMBER OF"
50    PRINT "KEY COMPONENTS IN EACH TRIAL AND THE"
60    PRINT "NUMBER OF TRIALS."
70    PRINT
80    INPUT "ENTER THE NUMBER OF KEY COMPONENTS";N
90    PRINT
100   INPUT "ENTER THE NUMBER OF TRIALS";NT
110   PRINT
120   DIM T$(NT,N),C(2 * N)
130   PRINT "RESULTS OF";NT;"TRIALS AND THE NUMBER OF HEADS"
140   FOR I = 1 TO NT
150   LET NH = 0
160   FOR J= 1 TO N
170   LET X = RND (1)
180   IF X < .5 THEN 220
190   T$ (I,J) = "H"
200   NH = NH + 1
210   GOTO 230
220   T$ (I,J) = "T"
230   IF J = N THEN 260
240   PRINT T$ (I,J);
250   GOTO 270
260   PRINT T$ (I,J);" ";NH,
270   NEXT J
280   C(NH + 1) = C(NH + 1) + 1
290   NEXT I
300   PRINT
310   PRINT
320   PRINT "# OF HEADS", "# OF TRIALS"
330   FOR K= 1 TO N + 1
340   PRINT K - 1,C(K)
350   NEXT K
360   END
```

Table 1
Computer Simulation for 100 Trials of Tossing a Coin 7 Times,
with Number of Heads Noted in Second Column

TTTTTHT	1	TTTTTTH	1	TTTHHHH	4	HHTTTHH	4
HTTTTHT	2	TTHHTTT	2	HTTHTHH	4	HHHTTTT	3
THHTTTT	2	THHHTTT	3	HHHHTHH	6	TTHHHHT	4
HHHHHTH	6	HTTTHHT	3	HTHHTHT	4	TTTTHHT	2
HTHHHHH	6	THTTHTT	2	HTTHHTH	4	TTHTHHH	4
TTHHHHH	5	THHHTTT	3	TTHHTHH	4	HHTHTTT	3
HTHHHHT	5	THTTHTH	3	HHHTHHT	5	HHTHTTT	3
THTTHHH	4	TTTHHHH	4	HHTTHHH	5	HHHHHHT	6
HHHHHTT	5	HTTTTHH	3	HTTHHHT	4	HHHTTTH	4
TTTHTHH	3	HHHHHTT	5	THTHTHT	3	TTHTTTH	2
HTHHTHT	4	HHHHTHT	5	HTTTHHT	3	HTHHHHT	5
HHHTTHH	5	HTTHTTT	2	HHTTTTH	3	HHTTHHH	5
TTTHHTH	3	HTTHHTH	4	HTTHTTT	2	THTTHTT	2
HHTTHTH	4	THHTTHT	3	THTHTTH	3	HTHTHHT	4
TTTTTHH	2	TTHHHTT	3	HTTTHTH	3	TTHTTTH	2
HTTTTTT	1	HHTHTTH	4	THHTHTH	4	HHHTTTT	3
THHTHHH	5	HHTHTTT	3	HHTTHTT	3	TTTTTTH	1
TTTTTHT	1	THTHHHT	4	TTTTHTT	1	TTHHHTM	4
THHTHHT	4	TTHHTTH	3	HTTHTHH	4	THTTHHT	3
HHHHTHH	6	HHTTTTT	2	TTHHHHT	4	HHHHTHT	5
HTHTHHH	5	HTHHTTT	3	HTHHHTT	4	HHTHTHT	4
HTHHTHH	5	HTHTHTT	3	HTTTTHT	2	HHTTTHH	4
HHHTTHH	5	HTHTTHH	4	HTTHTHH	4	THTHHTT	3
HTTHHTH	4	HTTTHHH	4	TTTHTTH	2	TTHHTHH	4
THHTHHT	4	TTTTHTT	1	HTTTTHT	2	TTHHTHT	3

Table 2
Summary of Table 1 Outcomes for Number of Heads Occurring per Trial
in 100 Trials of 7 Coin Tosses

Number of Heads per Trial	Number of Trials (7 Coin Tosses) with This Outcome	Estimated Probability
0	0	$\frac{0}{100}$
1	7	$\frac{7}{100}$
2	15	$\frac{15}{100}$
3	26	$\frac{26}{100}$
4	32	$\frac{32}{100}$
5	15	$\frac{15}{100}$
6	5	$\frac{5}{100}$
7	0	$\frac{0}{100}$

In Table 1, the numbers next to the outcomes of the seven key components show the number of heads and make the counting of heads easier. We see from the table that the first trial resulted in TTTTTHT. One head in the trial corresponds to Mary guessing only one answer correctly. Table 2 contains a summary of the numerical outcome of interest— the number of heads. We see that, in 100 trials, one head occurred 7 times, two heads occurred 15 times, and so on. The probability that Mary guesses four or more answers correctly is estimated by

$$\frac{(32 + 15 + 5 + 0)}{100} = \frac{52}{100} = 0.5, \text{ approximately}$$

You may be interested in knowing how close your simulation results are to the theoretical probabilities. The mathematical formula for these probabilities, in the case where each key component has only two possible outcomes denoted as *yes* and *no*, is as follows:

Let n = number of key components in each trial
k = number of *yes*es observed
p = probability of getting a *yes* as the outcome of a key component

Then, the probability of getting k *yes*es in n repeats of the key component is given by the formula

$$\frac{n(n-1)\,(n-2)\ldots(n-k+1)}{k(k-1)\,(k-2)\ldots 2 \times 1} \times p^k(1-p)^{n-k}$$

For example, the theoretical probability of seeing exactly k = 4 heads in a series of n = 7 coin tosses is

$$\frac{7\,(6)\,(5)\,(4)}{4\,(3)\,(2)\,(1)}\left(\frac{1}{2}\right)^4\left(\frac{1}{2}\right)^3 = 35\left(\frac{1}{2}\right)^7 = \frac{35}{128} = 0.27$$

which is close to our simulated result of $\frac{32}{100}$ = 0.32.

The average number of correct guesses for the seven-question exam is calculated from the formula

$$\frac{\text{number of trials favorable to } E}{\text{total number of trials}} =$$

$$\frac{1(7) + 2(15) + 3(26) + 4(32) + 5(15) + 6(5) + 7(0)}{100} = 3.48$$

Thus, we expect Mary to guess three or four answers correctly on a seven-question true–false exam.

In performing a large simulation using a coin-tossing model, it may be too time consuming actually to toss the coins the required number of times. In that case, Table 3 can be used. This table shows the results of 2,000 coin tosses. Just enter the table at any point and read up, down, left, or right to obtain random results for the required number of tosses.

We used a coin to generate the outcomes of our experiment because we wanted a device that would generate two outcomes with equal frequency. You do not have to use a coin. You can set up your own scheme for simulating results of a trial that can have only two possible outcomes. For example, you could use a die as your device. Since a toss of a die can result in six outcomes, three of them even and three of them odd, you could have the even numbers represent the result of your event of interest. You could also make your own spinner. The main thing to watch for is that the outcomes have an equal chance of occurring.

Here are two more examples of how to use the eight-step process.

Table 3
2,000 Tosses of a Coin

TTHTH	THHTH	THHTT	TTHTH	THHTT	HHTHT	HTHTH	TTTHT	TTHTT	HHTTH
THHTT	HHTHH	HTTTH	TTHHT	HHHTH	HHTTH	HTHHT	HTHHT	THTTT	TTTHT
TTHTT	HTTTT	TTTHH	TTTTH	HHHTH	HHHTH	HTHTH	HHTTT	THTTT	HTHHH
THHHH	THTTH	TTHHH	HHHHTH	HTTTH	HTHHH	TTTTT	HTHTH	THTTT	HHTHH
HHHTH	THTHH	THHHH	HHTTT	HTHHH	THTTH	HHTTH	HTHHH	HTHTH	THTHH
THTTH	THHTT	THHHT	TTTHH	HTTTH	THTHH	HTHTH	TTTHT	TTHHT	THTTT
HHHTH	THHTH	HHHTT	TTHHT	TTHHH	HHHTT	HTHTT	HHTTT	TTHHT	HTTTT
TTTTT	HTHHH	HTHHT	HTTHH	HTHHT	HTHHH	HTTHT	HTTTH	TTTHT	THTHT
HTTTT	TTTTT	THHHTH	HHHHT	HTTHH	HTTHT	HHHTT	HHHTT	TTTHT	TTHHT
THTHT	THTHT	HHHTT	HTTHT	TTTTT	THHHH	THTTH	THHTH	HHTTH	HHTTT
THHHT	HHHTH	HTTTT	TTTTH	HHTTH	THTHH	TTTHT	THHHT	TTTTT	HTHTT
TTHHT	THHTT	THTHH	THHHH	THHTH	TTTTH	TTTHH	HHTHT	HHTHH	THHHH
HTHTT	THTHH	TTHTT	THHHH	HTHTH	HHTHT	HHHTH	HHHTH	HTHTH	THHTT
TTHHH	TTHHT	HHHHT	HTTTH	HHHHHH	TTHTH	HTHHH	TTHTT	HHTHH	HTHTH
HTTHT	HTHHH	THTHH	THTHT	HTHTH	TTTTH	HHTTT	HTHHH	HHTHH	THTTH
THTTH	TTTTT	TTTTH	TTTTH	TTHHT	HTHTT	HTTTT	THHTT	THTHT	TTHTT
HTHTT	HHTHH	HHHTT	TTHTH	HHTHT	HHHTH	TTHHH	HTHHH	HHHHT	THHTH
HHTTT	HTHHT	THHTT	HTTTH	THTTH	TTHHT	TTTTT	HHHHH	HHHHH	HTTTT
HHHTH	TTHTT	TTTTH	HHTHT	HTTTH	TTHTH	THHHT	THHHH	TTTHT	TTHHT
HTHTH	THTHH	THHHT	THTTH	HHTHT	THTHH	THHTH	THTHH	THHHH	HTTTH
HTTTT	TTHHH	TTHHT	HHHTH	THTTH	THTTT	HTTHT	HTTTT	TTTHH	HTHTT
HHTHH	THHHT	HTHTH	THHTH	HTHHT	HTTTH	TTHHT	TTTTT	HHTTT	HTTHH
TTTTT	HHTTH	THTTT	HHHHT	THHHT	THTHH	TTTHT	HHHTT	HTTHT	HHTTH
HHTTH	TTTTH	HHTHT	HTTHH	THHTT	HHHTT	HHTHH	THTHT	THTTH	HTTHH
HHHHT	HTHHH	HTTTH	HHHHH	HHHTH	HHHTT	TTTHT	TTTHT	HTTTH	HHHTT
HTHHT	TTHHH	HTTHH	HHTHH	HTHTT	HTTTT	THTHT	HHHHT	THTTH	THTHT
TTHTT	HHTTH	HTTTT	TTHTT	THHHT	THTTT	HHHTT	HHHHH	TTHTT	HHHHH
THTHH	HTHTT	HTTTH	THHHH	THHHT	THTTH	HHHTH	THHHH	THTTH	HHHTH
TTHTT	HTHHH	TTHHT	TTTTH	TTTTT	TTTTH	TTHTT	HHHHH	HTTTT	HHTTH
HTHHH	HHTHT	THHTT	HTHHT	THTTT	THTTT	TTHHT	THTHH	TTHHT	TTHTT
THHHT	TTHHT	HHTTH	HHTHH	THHHH	THTHH	THHHH	TTHTT	HTTTH	HTHHT
HTHTT	HTHHH	THHTT	HTTTT	TTTTT	TTTHT	THTTT	TTTTT	THHTT	THTHT
HTTHT	THHHT	HTTTH	THTHT	HTHHH	TTTTT	THHHT	TTTTT	THHHH	HHHHH
HTTTH	HHHHH	THTHT	HTHHT	HHHTT	TTHHT	THTHT	THHHH	THTHH	HTTTT
HTHHT	TTTTH	HHTHH	HHTTH	TTTHH	HTHTT	THTHT	TTHHT	TTHTH	HTHTT
TTTTH	HTHTT	TTTHT	HHTHH	HHHHH	HHTHT	THTTT	HTTHT	HTHHT	THTTH
TTTTT	TTTTH	HHHHH	TTTHT	HHTTH	TTTHH	HHTTH	HTTTT	HTHHH	HHTHH
TTHHH	TTHHT	THHHH	HTHTH	HTTTT	THTHT	HTHTH	HHHHT	THTHT	TTTHH
HTHHH	HTTHH	HHHTH	HTHHH	THTTH	THHHH	HHTTH	THTHH	HTTHH	TTHTT
HHTTT	THHTT	THHHT	HTTTT	THTHT	THHHT	TTHHH	HHHHT	HTHTT	HTTTT

Example 1

Step 1   State the problem clearly.

What is the probability that a three-child family will contain exactly one girl?

Step 2   Define the key components.

A key component is the birth of one child, which may be either a boy or a girl.

Step 3   State the underlying assumptions.

We assume that the probability of the birth of a female child is one half and that the sex of a child is independent of the sex of any other child.

Step 4   Select a model to generate the outcomes for a key component.

We will toss a coin and let heads correspond to a female birth. (We could also use a die and let an even number correspond to a female birth, or we could use a random number table and let digits 0 through 4 correspond to a female birth.)

Step 5   Define and conduct a trial.

We will toss a coin three times to represent a three-child family. The first trial (set of three coin tosses) turned out to be HHT, which corresponds to two girls and one boy being born into the family.

Step 6   Record the observation of interest.

We are interested only in whether or not exactly one girl was born into the three-child family. The first trial (HHT) was *not* favorable to the event of interest.

Step 7   Repeat steps 5 and 6 until 50 trials are reached.

The results of 50 trials are shown below. Asterisks mark those trials favorable to the event "exactly one girl."

HHT	THH	HHH	THT*	HTT*
TTT	THT*	HTH	THH	HTH
HHH	HHH	HHT	THH	HTH
HTT*	HHH	HTH	HHT	THH
HHH	THT*	TTT	TTT	TTH*
HTT*	HTH	HTT*	THT*	THH
HHT	HHH	HTT*	HHH	HHH
TTT	THT*	HTH	TTT	TTT
TTH*	HHT	HTH	TTT	HHT
THH	THT*	HTT*	THT*	HHH

Step 8   Summarize the information and draw conclusions.

There are 15 trials favorable to the event of interest. Therefore, the probability of seeing exactly one girl in a three-child family is estimated to be $\frac{15}{50}$ = 0.30.

Example 2

Step 1 State the problem clearly.

Our new neighbor has two children, but I do not know their sex. However, I am told that there is at least one girl in the family. What is the probability that there are two girls in the family?

Step 2 Define the key components.

A key component is the birth of a child, which may be either a boy or a girl.

Step 3 State the underlying assumptions.

We assume that the probability of the birth of a female child is one half and that the sex of one child is independent of the sex of the other child.

Step 4 Select a model for a key component.

We will toss a coin and let heads correspond to a female birth.

Step 5 Define and conduct a trial.

We toss a coin twice since there are two children in the family. However, if two tails come up, we do *not* count the toss as a trial. At least one head must appear because we *know* that there is at least one girl in the family. Our first trial was HT, which we can keep in our simulation because an H occurred.

Step 6 Record the observation of interest.

The observation in this example is simply whether or not two heads (two girls) appear on the trial. The first trial (HT) was *not* favorable to this event.

Step 7 Repeat steps 5 and 6 until 50 trials are reached.

The results of 50 trials are shown in the following display. Asterisks mark the trials favorable to the event "two girls."

HT	HT	HH*	TH	TH
HH*	HH*	TH	HH*	HH*
HT	HH*	HH*	HT	HT
HT	TH	HH*	TH	HH*
HH*	TH	TH	HT	HH*
TH	HH*	HT	TH	TH
HH*	TH	HH*	TH	HT
TH	HH*	HH*	HH*	TH
TH	HH*	TH	TH	HT
HT	HT	HH*	TH	HT

Step 8 Summarize the information and draw conclusions.

It is seen that 19 of the 50 trials are favorable to the event of interest. Therefore, our estimate of the probability that there are two girls in the family, when we know that there is at least one girl, is $\frac{19}{50} = 0.38$.

Now apply the eight-step procedure to the following problems.

Application 1

The Passing Game

A quarterback on a football team completes 50 percent of his passes. Suppose he makes 10 passes in a game. Use a simulation model to find the following estimates.

1. Estimate the probability that he completes all passes.

2. Estimate the probability that he completes exactly five passes.

3. Estimate the probability that he completes at least five passes.

4. What number of completions, per 10 passes in a game, is most likely?

5. Guess his average number of completions per game without using simulation.

6. Calculate the average number of completions per game from your simulation. Is this average close to your answer to question 5?

$$\left(\text{average number of completions} = \frac{\text{sum of number of completions}}{\text{number of trials}}\right)$$

(*Hint:* In this simulation, the probability of the quarterback completing any one pass is one half. This probability is assumed to remain the same for each pass, and the outcome of any one pass is assumed to be independent of those that preceded it. A total of at least 50 trials should be run in the simulation, but these could be combined from more than one student.)

All That Jazz

John decides to set up a jazz group with his seven best friends. The group will work only if at least five of his friends can join. Using simulation, answer the following questions.

1. If John thinks that there is a 50 percent chance that each of his friends will join the group, can you estimate the probability of getting at least five friends to join the group?

2. Do you think John is being too ambitious in planning a group of at least five?

3. What is the most likely size of his group? (That is, what number that will join, out of the seven, has the highest estimated probability?)

(*Hint:* You could use the simulation results from the series of true–false questions in Tables 1 and 2 to answer these questions.)

Application 3

Aardvarks Versus Bears

Two evenly matched baseball teams, team A and team B, are to play a five-game series. All five games are played, no matter who wins. For simplicity, we assume that the outcome of any one game is independent of the outcomes of any games that might have preceded it. Use simulation to answer the following questions.

1. Find the probability that team A wins three or more games and thereby wins the series.

2. Find the probability that either team A or team B wins four or more games.

3. Find the probability that no team wins two or more games in a row.

4. Estimate the number of games you would expect team A to win in such a five-game series.

5. What number of wins for team A has the highest probability of occurring?

(*Hint:* In this simulation, team A has a probability of one half of winning any one game since the teams are evenly matched. The outcome of one game can be simulated by a coin toss, with heads denoting "team A wins the game." You can use Table 3 to get the outcome of a coin toss.)

The Water System

The diagram below describes the five aging pumping stations and the water-main system for a city. At any particular time, the probability of pump failure at each pumping station is 0.5. For water to flow from A to B, both pumps in at least one path must be working. For example, if pumps 1 and 2 are working, water will flow. If pumps 2 and 3 are working, water will flow. If pumps 2 and 4 are *not* working, water will not flow. Simulate the pumping operation and answer the following questions.

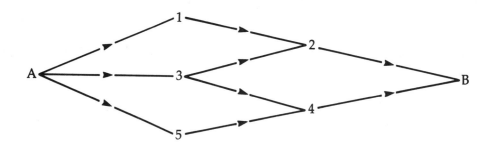

1. Estimate the probability that water will flow from A to B at any particular time.

2. On the average, how many stations were working at any time, according to your simulation?

3. Estimate the probability that the 1–2 path is working at any time.

(*Hint:* It is now important to keep track of which pumps are working. You might let **five** different students represent the five pumps. Each tosses one coin, with heads representing "the pump works." Then, observe whether or not there is at least one working path from A to B. Water will flow if you get two or more heads in sequence in five coin tosses. Note also that each trial must be counted only once, even if more than one path is open. Repeat the tosses for more trials. Combine the data with other groups of students until at least 50 trials are conducted.)

III. SIMULATION WHEN PROBABILITIES DIFFER FROM ONE HALF

In the examples that we have discussed so far, we have generated the outcomes of our experiments and trials by tossing a coin. We did this because each of the outcomes had an equal chance of happening. Suppose we had a key component that could result in three outcomes, all of them equally likely to take place. The coin would not be the appropriate device in this case. We need some device that will generate one of three numbers without favoring any one of them. There are several devices one can use to accomplish this. We will describe three such devices in this section. You may be able to think of some others yourself.

Spinner

You have all played games that have used spinners. You can make one yourself by following these steps:

A. Draw a circle on a piece of cardboard. Divide the circle into as many equal parts as the number of outcomes. Number each part. If we have three outcomes, then we would divide the circle into three equal parts. (*Hint:* You will need a compass for this.)

B. Take a large paper clip and a sharp pencil. Hold one end of the clip in place at the center of the circle using the tip of the pencil. Spin the other end of the clip and note where it stops. You have now obtained a random number.

Die

Another device you can use is a die. A die has six faces, each with a different number on it, and every time you toss a die, any one of the six faces can be on the top. That means that each of the six numbers has an equal chance of being the number on the top face of the die. See if you can figure out how to use a die to simulate a trial with either two, three, or six outcomes. You may refer to Table 4 (page 16) instead of actually tossing a die.

The dodecahedral die is a die with 12 faces. A dodecahedral die is a useful device to use when 12 outcomes are equally likely. Think about how you might use a dodecahedral die when two, three, four, or six outcomes are equally likely. You may refer to Table 5 (page 17) instead of actually tossing a dodecahedral die. In Table 5, we use the number 0 to represent an outcome of 10, the letter *a* to represent an outcome of 11, and the letter *b* to represent an outcome of 12.

Regular Die

Dodecahedral Die

Table 4
Table of Random Numbers from 1 to 6 Simulating 2,000 Throws of a Regular Die

22212	26352	56651	34314	56215	14453	14662	23224	65354	16664
12415	15552	23426	21231	32432	42526	12562	44664	65436	35464
36551	44222	33121	36121	41615	42115	65445	23222	25241	13333
31552	32655	23655	41311	62642	53314	54514	24355	42555	56351
23514	53141	12444	66246	15634	13151	54541	54341	51321	66144
43265	63546	15164	45546	42162	54232	43143	16663	46253	55665
25363	23343	31462	26134	35333	44632	24634	54561	51565	63526
32311	22213	63121	35255	35336	13531	32461	22346	32235	26353
15416	54541	22632	55614	26543	63255	44662	65632	31433	36423
14255	21451	23564	42463	21244	65222	14565	46532	45313	35451
43623	31264	45635	14121	63252	36453	43454	53114	12254	35151
36425	51555	65426	34525	22425	34641	56162	42444	31232	65331
12356	42164	33251	34512	51412	34326	15213	11315	56351	24662
52444	25262	51452	55254	24233	52254	21223	36616	44224	52313
14532	62522	62532	64445	21426	63116	16365	15261	26352	44512
46216	55534	54264	41432	35565	43111	42524	44656	52261	62464
33646	52544	15662	32424	21323	52354	56545	24156	31132	12353
26461	44564	23643	16325	34563	23442	21422	26513	35113	24633
42131	41436	24443	63453	46656	12541	32614	54513	51352	34164
63533	22111	35511	33344	63656	55213	24626	14156	25456	24143
36261	52416	62663	16412	44525	11561	26146	51136	66531	42421
35244	55231	24525	56466	13433	14534	42145	43443	56624	34561
21614	26362	33265	65245	56663	63631	44342	64655	41322	32111
13621	35363	15536	61566	33425	64541	51156	34316	34556	15115
42141	26564	54215	45424	24655	55565	46114	16565	15352	56314
42524	64442	15624	54224	63426	61366	16122	52225	51111	15521
56113	12124	33111	13554	55553	65135	64562	15363	23456	53311
15555	35611	11314	63631	12522	32541	14524	43363	34322	25224
34364	62151	41423	52545	66522	51433	42563	62153	22163	16166
53215	36451	34221	24556	62133	14352	55416	52333	54243	12521
25446	64511	12443	11543	61163	65552	42134	16245	31452	64341
54245	41443	15125	41463	14534	16641	35356	43114	53335	52323
34663	26566	32565	53334	61523	15622	61141	43655	55246	31551
66162	13421	46652	65453	31363	33536	44414	21466	12213	11143
45633	63221	31542	44224	12345	64342	64542	46635	35613	22135
23566	65522	25122	26255	22442	15613	54225	33113	25312	25541
36314	13244	31254	62551	53223	24264	13446	66416	23412	65534
16536	12363	46616	62326	46521	41655	45422	24236	11441	15516
33632	66322	53121	31645	45211	15443	25351	13644	63641	43656
42465	66126	44535	11223	21631	12326	26213	43265	11132	13442

Table 5
Table of Random Numbers from 1 to 12 Simulating 2,000 Tosses of a Dodecahedral Die
(0 = 10, a = 11, b = 12)

64b73	b1ba1	b7730	61528	7b948	4913b	5a941	77a67	25250	00167
64867	89428	b4275	21b31	98b19	8a15b	51246	07b32	56589	85a58
53577	28907	82709	44ab6	1b1a3	a8746	29a30	a7779	154a3	381b6
86311	66b65	8ba32	2500b	91024	4856a	079aa	16014	3749a	85527
97434	48916	8ab79	19b4b	18984	68b00	46424	46900	3b998	b1218
586a9	831b6	b7b34	72468	17a22	747a8	3a0a2	47617	1635a	b3b58
65824	40342	b04a5	aa938	357b0	32661	05966	68484	37b39	98341
a9325	81415	88b05	69359	330b3	516a0	83a82	98965	42219	b0a5b
07818	80447	485a8	603a3	a99a0	509b1	55696	98319	47930	94821
a7171	59170	98aaa	32a78	1ba60	760b9	292a8	89458	71b81	aa299
46018	38558	a9155	67931	b1570	13985	87092	6a431	8987a	466b1
89a58	55493	27030	44b54	87325	9086a	8a647	8372b	27688	4b341
43b69	60415	b7908	32228	5b543	13387	23801	978b9	00892	03098
08597	74421	4458a	17542	97909	36b28	7b304	670a6	694b6	7b20b
025ab	a3792	5948a	281bb	86293	46940	3a656	4012a	44120	9a4a1
32bb3	90845	89b7a	104b2	55a48	b0283	b04a6	98685	74bb6	972a8
88652	31740	57a8a	40b63	8029b	bb927	64a66	a4658	22642	43845
23758	b5922	8b75b	2b758	11995	b4460	64924	36136	40111	4aa28
b87a9	23a42	87272	00636	58a7a	7a873	32370	62608	4b217	90801
4b023	25075	91375	aa7b2	1b761	60a89	b041b	667b4	859a8	a0600
63103	64383	38849	33324	96158	5b566	6a78b	64405	46864	15855
9007b	96b05	ab50b	67491	0b986	24777	6b168	08589	09089	68896
795a1	82331	69b45	65396	26b61	a55a3	87988	14192	15b53	17806
25712	87a09	4867a	798b5	80818	56814	90035	132b3	5b303	b3442
57089	89978	6a452	61596	10850	2420b	87978	97290	6799a	99711
89824	47943	3bb46	63850	71aa5	62b96	09b52	2b212	22391	67925
62a70	508b6	14480	5614a	06a62	6101b	0219b	b7549	75360	00994
14930	36165	b622b	9b264	8118a	70956	a6335	9ba81	92253	29193
a7abb	496ba	8736a	1b39a	90b99	88bb9	03024	72574	24917	59996
68885	33a67	54171	3919a	47a29	6a813	697a0	4a87a	284a1	a7106
32b8b	b295a	92247	b241b	43971	2b5a4	8324a	7a6b4	aa308	95532
37572	53a25	109bb	a8510	04298	87113	2b91b	90195	49201	56957
9a695	00249	35507	63982	8b301	ab401	b8a65	50881	b4271	6b308
31592	15117	49b89	287b2	2bb90	62464	7b2b7	b4779	731a9	50791
30874	19a71	7b116	71605	29099	35885	350a5	713a1	53b95	82800
08173	82603	92281	b109a	a2782	07797	9a435	ab679	02795	4602a
93818	7483a	85b61	376b1	43a65	964a4	16174	51512	80015	12786
48b86	27168	1246a	358b5	37108	2462a	25215	0137a	b5830	b0459
1b6a9	5911a	6b584	a3203	65277	47969	39198	6b92a	37358	3a663
a7453	0b805	57070	6804b	07924	99330	28736	93586	45291	94714

Random Number Tables

Suppose the digits from 0 through 9 are written on ten chips, one number per chip, and placed in a box. The chips are mixed, and one is drawn out without the number being seen. The number selected is called a *random number*, or *random digit*, because it is equally likely to have any value from 0 to 9. By replacing that chip and repeating the selection process, a second random number can be drawn. If this process is repeated many times, a table of random numbers like Table 6 can be formed.

Most random number tables are generated by a computer, but they have the same result as drawing numbers out of a box. Each number drawn is equally likely to take on any of the ten possible values, and the draws are independent of each other.

Consider a key component with ten possible outcomes (like selecting one of ten students to serve on a committee). We can simulate this component by using a random number table. First, number the students from 0 to 9. Second, enter the random number table at any random point. (You may just drop your pencil onto the table and take the number closest to its point.) Third, select the student whose number matches the number selected from the table. We have, by this method, *randomly* selected one student from the ten.

A trial may consist of more than one such key component. For example, three different classes of size ten may each be selecting one person for the committee. We can find three random numbers by locating a random starting point and then reading a series of three numbers going up, down, right, or left on the table. (We do not need to have three different random starting points.)

Random number tables can be used to generate the results of a trial with almost any probability structure. For example, suppose a salesman makes a sale to 35 percent of the customers. We could simulate the result of a contact with a customer by using these tables. Since the salesman makes a sale to 35 out of 100 customers, we can let the first 35 two-digit numbers (00, 01, . . ., 34) represent a sale. This means that, if we read a two-digit number from the table and it is *less than* 35, then it is a sale. (Note that 00 must be included as a possible number.) Table 6 gives 2,000 random digits grouped for convenience into groups of five digits. Suppose we start at the eleventh row of Table 6 and on the eleventh and twelfth columns, reading down. The first five two-digit numbers are 76, 37, 05, 10, 95. So, we now have results of five key components: no sale, no sale, sale, sale, no sale—or two sales in five contacts.

These are only some of the ways you can generate random numbers of any size. If you have a microcomputer available to you, you can probably generate these numbers yourself using a random number generator function that is built into the computer.

Table 6									
2,000 Random Digits from 0 to 9									
78086	27605	80783	72059	05060	21366	84811	80730	77042	25406
36673	74153	37788	35736	83780	11566	25916	85274	27965	27549
09752	89231	06739	64351	80303	47999	15059	00677	46402	98961
58358	21124	08164	56928	95491	80511	23897	96281	19001	42952
89928	22964	26249	90286	41979	64737	99888	81369	22711	40318
49390	91663	94701	66328	08696	43795	13916	65570	73393	43882
22219	93199	21573	13645	72126	38799	89648	26301	80918	55096
28034	42119	88853	07211	56700	59113	84358	86127	94675	99511
58449	34746	64619	19171	63533	97899	84381	65023	80908	18694
10920	69975	82955	27251	43127	99059	25076	48299	71133	60036
36422	93239	76046	81114	77412	86557	19549	98473	15221	87856
78496	47197	37961	67568	14861	61077	85210	51264	49975	71785
95384	59596	05081	39968	80495	00192	94679	18307	16265	48888
37957	89199	10816	24260	52302	69592	55019	94127	71721	70673
31422	27529	95051	83157	96377	33723	52902	51302	86370	50452
07443	15346	40653	84238	24430	88834	77318	07486	33950	61598
41349	86255	92715	96656	49693	99286	83447	20215	16040	41085
12398	95111	45663	55020	57159	58010	43162	98878	73337	35571
77229	92095	44305	09285	73256	02968	31129	66588	48126	52700
61175	53014	60304	13976	96312	42442	96713	43940	92516	81421
16825	27482	97858	05642	88047	68960	52991	67703	29805	42701
84656	03089	05166	67571	25545	26603	40243	55482	38341	97781
03872	31767	23729	89523	73654	24625	78393	77172	41328	95633
40488	70426	04034	46618	55102	93408	10965	69744	80766	14889
98322	25528	438087	05935	78338	77881	90139	72375	50624	91385
13366	52764	02407	14202	74172	58770	65348	24115	44277	96735
86711	27764	86789	43800	87582	09298	17880	75507	35217	08352
53886	50358	62738	91783	71944	90221	79403	75139	09102	77826
99348	21186	42266	01531	44325	61942	13453	61917	90426	12437
49985	08787	59448	82680	52929	19077	98518	06251	58451	91140
49807	32863	69984	20102	09523	47827	08374	79849	19352	62726
46569	00365	23591	44317	55054	94835	20633	66215	46668	53587
09988	44203	43532	54538	16619	45444	11957	69184	98398	96508
32916	00567	82881	59753	54761	39404	90756	91760	18698	42852
93285	32297	27254	27198	99093	97821	46277	10439	30389	45372
03222	39951	12738	50303	25017	84207	52123	88637	19369	58289
87002	61789	96250	99337	14144	00027	53542	87030	14773	73087
68840	94259	01961	52552	91843	33855	00824	48733	81297	80411
88323	28828	64765	08244	53077	50897	91937	08871	91517	19668
55170	71962	64159	79364	53088	21536	39451	95649	65256	23950

Example

Step 1   State the problem clearly.

Jo drives a minibus in her town. The bus has eight seats. People buy tickets in advance, but, on the average, 10 percent of those who buy tickets do not show up. So Jo sells 10 tickets for each trip. Sometimes more than eight people show up with tickets. Estimate the probability that this will happen.

Step 2   Define the key components.

The key components here are whether or not each person holding a ticket shows up for the trip.

Step 3   State the underlying assumptions.

The probability that any one person with a ticket fails to show up for the trip is 0.1. A ticketholder showing up or not showing up is independent of what other ticketholders do.

Step 4   Select a model for a key component.

We will draw a number from a random number table. The number 0 will represent a ticketholder who did *not* show up for the trip.

Step 5   Define and conduct a trial.

Since 10 tickets are sold for each trip, one trial will consist of drawing 10 random numbers. These numbers represent the ticketholders for one trip.

Our first trial resulted in the numbers 0, 6, 4, 9, 3, 1, 8, 6, 6, 9, which means that 9 of the 10 ticketholders showed up for the trip.

Step 6   Record the observation of interest.

Since nine ticketholders showed up, one did not get a seat. We can easily keep track of the number of ticketholders who did not get seats for each trip.

Step 7   Repeat steps 5 and 6 until 100 trials are completed.

The results of 100 such trials are summarized as follows:

Number Not Getting Seats	Number of Trials
0	26
1	31
2	43

Step 8 Summarize the information and draw conclusions.

The data from step 7 show that more than eight people showed up 74 times out of 100. Therefore, the probability that more than eight ticketholders show up for any one trip is estimated to be $\frac{74}{100} = 0.74$.

Also, the average number of people not getting seats per trip is

$$\frac{0(26) + 1(31) + 2(43)}{100} = \frac{117}{100} = 1.17$$

On the average, Jo can expect between one and two unhappy customers for each trip she makes!

Traffic Lights

Coming to school each day, Anne rides through three traffic lights, A, B, and C. The probability that any one light is green is 0.3, and the probability that it is *not* green is 0.7. Use a simulation to answer questions 1 and 2 below.

1. Estimate the probability that Anne will find all traffic lights to be green.

2. Estimate the probability that Anne will find at least one light to be not green.

3. Calculate the theoretical probability that Anne will find all three lights to be green, assuming that the lights operate independently. Compare this answer with your answer to question 1.

(*Hint:* We assume that the lights operate independently. For any one light, the probability that it is green when Anne arrives can be simulated by drawing a random digit from Table 6 and letting "green" be represented by the numbers 0, 1, 2. Drawing a number from 3 through 9 will represent the light not being green.)

Application 6

Working Women

Assume that the percentage of women in the labor force of a certain country is 30 percent. A company employs ten workers, two of whom are women.

1. What is the probability that this would occur by chance? (Estimate the probability by a simulation.)

2. Estimate the probability that a company of ten workers would employ two or *fewer* women, by chance.

3. Estimate the expected number of women that a company of ten workers would employ, making use of your simulation results.

4. In simulating the number of women among the ten workers, what number occurs most frequently?

5. On the basis of your simulation, do you think that women are underrepresented in the company? Why or why not?

(*Hint:* Selecting a female worker by chance means that any one worker employed has a 0.3 probability of being a woman. Assume that the pool of workers is large, so that this probability of 0.3 does not change when a few workers are removed from the pool.)

Random Ties

A man has 10 ties and chooses a tie at random to wear to work each day. Set up a simulation to answer the following questions.

1. Estimate the probability that he wears the same tie more than once in a five-day week.

2. Estimate the probability that he wears the same tie more than twice in a five-day week.

3. Estimate the probability that he wears two different ties more than once each in a five-day week.

(*Hint:* You might simulate this situation by numbering the ties from 0 through 9. Then, select 5 random digits to represent the 5 ties randomly selected through the week. Repeat the simulation for 50 trials, preferably by working in groups.)

Application 8

What's Your Sign?

1. Estimate the probability that, in a group of five people, at least two of them have the same zodiacal sign. (There are 12 zodiacal signs; assume that each sign is equally likely for any person.)

2. Estimate the probability that at least one of the five people has the same zodiacal sign as yours.

(*Hint:* For a trial of this simulation, you must randomly choose 5 numbers from 12 possibilities. Two-digit numbers between 00 and 11 could be selected from a random number table, with each number—00, 01, 02, . . ., 11—representing one of the zodiacal signs.)

Multiple Choice

A multiple-choice test consists of ten questions, and each question has four possible answers, only one of which is correct. Using simulation, find answers to the questions below.

1. What is the probability of answering at least three questions correctly, if I guess all the answers?

2. Suppose it is always possible to eliminate one answer as being incorrect. If I guess from the remaining three answers, what is the probability of getting at least three answers correct on the test?

3. On the average, how many questions will a student answer correctly by guessing? (Assume that the student is always guessing from among the four choices.)

Application 10

Waiting in Line

A local bank has two teller windows open to serve customers. The number of customers arriving at the bank varies between one and six customers per minute. Customers form a line, and the person at the head of the line goes to the first available teller. Each teller services one customer per minute. Design a simulation for one 20-minute period, and record the number of people in the waiting line at the end of each minute. Use a table like the following:

Minute	Number Arriving	Number Waiting in Line	Waiting Time for Last Person
1	3	1	1 minute
2	4	3	2 minutes

1.   What is the length of the waiting line after the first five minutes?

2.   What is the time a person has to wait if he or she arrives on the tenth minute?

3.   How many times was the waiting time reduced to zero?

4.   What is the average number of people waiting in line over the 20-minute period?

5.   If you were the manager of the bank, would you increase or decrease the number of tellers? Repeat the simulation with one teller and with three tellers, and give your recommendation on the number of tellers that will make the average waiting time not more than 3 minutes.

Shooting Free Throws

Time has run out in the big basketball game, and the score is tied. However, the high school's best free-throw shooter, who has made a basket in 75 percent of her throws, was fouled and gets two shots after a short time-out. What is the probability that she will make at least one shot out of the two and win the game?

1. Hold a paper clip in place with the tip of your pencil and spin the spinner. What does the spin represent? Did she make the first shot?

2. The foul shooter gets another try. Spin again. This completes one trial. Did she break the tie?

3. Record the results of 30 such trials, and estimate the probability that the game is won on these shots.

Application 12

To Walk or Not to Walk?

You have a choice between walking to school and taking a bus. If you walk, the amount of time you take depends on the traffic and the weather conditions. Suppose the time needed to walk to school can be shown by the following diagram:

Time to walk
— 60 percent of the days it is 5 minutes.
— 40 percent of the days it is 8 minutes.

How about the time when you take the bus? You find that the time taken by the bus is as follows:

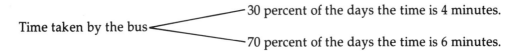

Time taken by the bus
— 30 percent of the days the time is 4 minutes.
— 70 percent of the days the time is 6 minutes.

What is your decision in this case? To get the answer, you can go through the following steps:

1. Find the total time taken if you walk for the five days of the week. Our key component is the time taken to walk on a single day. We will simulate an event by using a random number table. Since our probabilities are 0.6 and 0.4 for the two times, we can look for numbers between 0 and 9. We can then say that, for any day, if the number generated is between 0 and 5, which are 6 out of 10 possible digits, then the time will be 5 minutes, whereas if the number generated is between 6 and 9, then the time will be 8 minutes. We have started the table for you and have given the results for the first five trials using the random number table and starting with the first digit from column 6 and row 6. Complete the simulation and then calculate the average total time taken to walk for a week.

Numbers Generated	Time Taken	Total Time
9, 9, 4, 3, 6	8, 8, 5, 5, 8	34
9, 4, 5, 8, 2	8, 5, 5, 8, 5	31
1, 8, 9, 9, 5	5, 8, 8, 8, 5	34
2, 0, 3, 7, 2	5, 5, 5, 8, 5	28
5, 2, 5, 2, 0	5, 5, 5, 5, 5	25

2. Repeat the simulation for the bus. What is the average total time taken by the bus?

3. What have you decided? Is it worth taking the bus?

IV. SIMULATION WITH AN UNKNOWN NUMBER OF KEY COMPONENTS

All the examples and Applications that we have investigated up to this point have had trials with a fixed number of key components. But sometimes the length of a trial changes from trial to trial. We illustrate this case with one example, followed by more Applications of this type of problem.

Example

Step 1 State the problem clearly.

A cereal manufacturer includes a gift coupon in each box of a certain brand. These coupons can be exchanged for a gift when a complete set of six coupons has been collected. What is the expected number of boxes of cereal you will have to buy before you obtain a complete set of six coupons?

Step 2 Define the key components.

A key component consists of buying a box of cereal and observing which coupon it contains.

Step 3 State the underlying assumptions.

Since no other information on the distribution of coupons is given, we will assume that the six coupons occur with equal frequency. The coupon obtained in one box of cereal is independent of the outcomes for other boxes.

Step 4 Select a model for a key component.

We will number the six different coupons from 1 to 6. Since each is equally likely to be present in any one box, we model the outcome of one purchased box by rolling a die and observing the number that comes up. The number on the die corresponds to the coupon number.

Step 5 Define and conduct a trial.

A trial consists of rolling a die until a complete set of numbers (1, 2, 3, 4, 5, 6) is obtained. Our first trial was 4, 5, 1, 3, 1, 1, 1, 1, 6, 5, 3, 6, 6, 1, 3, 6, 3, 5, 3, 6, 4, 5, 4, 1, 1, 4, 1, 5, 4, 1, 6, 3, 6, 2, which took 34 tosses of the die.

Step 6 Record the observation of interest.

The observation of interest is the number of die tosses necessary to obtain a complete set of six numbers. For our first trial, this number was 34.

Step 7 Repeat steps 5 and 6 until at least 50 trials are completed.

We actually completed 200 trials. The second trial gave 4, 2, 4, 3, 4, 1, 6, 5, for a total of only eight tosses of the die. Other trials ranged from 6 to 39 tosses.

Step 8 Summarize the information and draw conclusions.

We performed 200 trials with an average of approximately 15 die tosses per trial. This average forms an estimate of the expected number of boxes of cereal you will have to buy in order to get a complete set of coupons.

Application 13

Mouse Maze

Have you heard of psychologists doing experiments to find out how animals learn? Some of these experiments involve mice who are put in a maze, with food at an exit point of this maze. Suppose an experiment is run with the following maze. A mouse is dropped into the maze at point A, with an exit at the center of the maze at B. The mouse will reach the exit only if it makes a right turn. Suppose our mouse were to take the first right turn every time. Does that mean that we have a "smart" mouse? Or could it be that the mouse was making the turns at random and was just lucky?

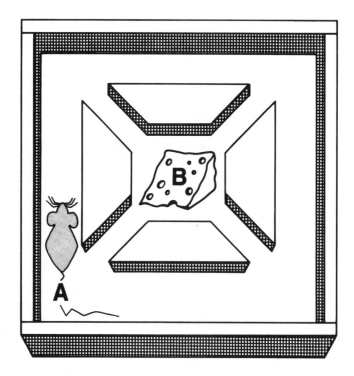

You can answer these questions by using simulation to find the probabilities that the mouse will reach the exit after passing 0, 1, 2, . . . turns. Toss a coin to simulate whether a mouse will make a right turn or keep going. Then record the number of tosses until the mouse reaches the exit. You should assume that the mouse cannot turn around in the maze.

Answer the following questions using simulation. Make sure that you carefully list your assumptions.

1. What is your estimate of the probability of the mouse making a right turn at the first chance?

2. What is your estimate of the probability that the mouse goes around the maze once (that is, passes four intersections) and then makes the very first right turn possible?

3. What is the maximum number of times the mouse will miss the right turn?

4. Do you think that a maze like this one would be very useful for finding out if animals learn from experience? Why or why not?

Donating Blood

In the United States, 45 percent of the people have type O blood. These people are called universal donors since their blood can be used in transfusions to people of any blood type. Assuming that donors arrive independently and randomly at a local blood bank, use simulation to answer the following questions.

1. If 10 donors came to a particular station in one day, what is the probability of at least four having type O blood?

2. On a certain day, a blood center needs four donors with O blood. How many donors, on the average, should they have to see in order to obtain exactly four with type O blood?

3. For your simulation of question 2, what was the maximum number of donors seen in order to find the first four type O donors? What was the minimum number? What number occurred most frequently?

(*Hint:* There are two kinds of simulations required in this activity. The simulation for question 1 is the kind discussed in Section III. The simulation for question 2 is the type considered in this section.)

Application 15

Drilling for Oil

Suppose the probability that an exploratory oil well will strike oil is about 0.2 and that each exploratory well costs $5,000 to drill. Conduct a simulation to find solutions to the following problems. Assume that the outcome (oil or no oil) for any one exploratory well is independent of outcomes for other wells that may have been drilled previously.

1. Estimate the average number of wells drilled *before* finding oil.

2. In your simulation, what was the maximum number of wells drilled, including the first successful one?

3. What is the average cost of exploration up to and including the first successful well drilled?

(*Hint:* In figuring the cost of exploration, keep in mind that the first successful well costs $5,000 to drill as well as each of the unsuccessful ones. You can find the answer to question 3 by using the solution for question 1.)

Family Planning

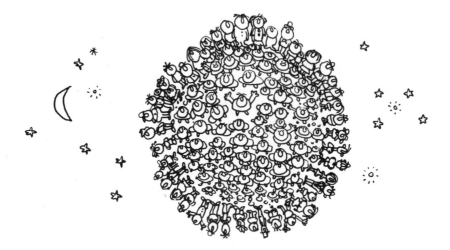

In many countries around the world, couples look to a son to take care of them in their old age. They therefore are inclined to keep having children until they have a son. Governments in overpopulated countries, such as China and India, would like to discourage this practice. However, suppose a government permits people to continue having children until they have exactly one son. Use simulation to answer the questions below.

1. What is the average number of children per family?

2. What is the average number of girls per family?

3. If the government wishes to keep its population from growing, should the government change its policy?

Application 17

Breaking the Bank

You have been playing well at a casino and have $10,000; the bank has $2,000 left. You are playing a game in which your probability of a win is 0.4, and you are making $1,000 bets. Design a simulation and run it until either you or the bank goes broke. Obtain the following data.

1. How often does the bank go broke?

2. How often do you go broke?

3. What is the average number of games you play before you go broke?

4. Are any of your answers surprising? What do you think affects the answers to questions 1, 2, and 3 more, the amount you start with or the probability of winning?

Waiting for the Bus

You are waiting for a bus in a very busy bus terminal. Fifty buses will come by within the next half hour, and any one of four of them can take you to your destination. Assume that the buses arrive in random order. Construct a simulation for bus arrivals, and use the simulation to answer the following questions.

1. How many buses do you expect to see arrive *before* the first one that will take you to your destination?

2. What did you observe to be the maximum number of buses that arrived before you saw a bus that will take you to your destination?

3. What is the probability that you can find a bus to take you to your destination among the first five arrivals?

(*Hint:* For this simulation, you know that there are four specified objects—your buses—among the 50. This could be modeled by using a deck of 50 cards with the four aces representing your buses. Mix the cards and count down from the top until the first ace is reached. This completes one trial of a simulation.)

V. SIMULATING MORE COMPLEX EVENTS

In many cases, a situation under study may have more than one characteristic of interest. For example, a Democratic candidate in an election may be interested not only in the number of registered Democrats but also in how many of the Democrats vote for him or her. Assume for the moment that all voters can be classified as Democrats or Republicans and that there are equal numbers of voters registered as Democrats and Republicans. Each voter now has two characteristics, the party he or she belongs to and the candidate he or she prefers. Suppose, historically in this district, 75 percent of the Democrats vote along party lines, whereas 80 percent of the Republicans vote along party lines. We now have the following information:

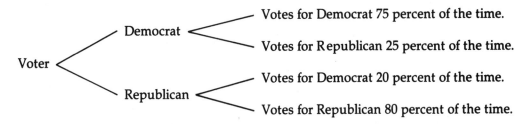

Our objective here is to find the number of voters voting for each of the two candidates. Let us go through the steps.

Step 1 The objective in this simulation is to determine the number of votes that the Democratic candidate gets.

Step 2 The situation is a combination of two key components, the party that a voter belongs to and the candidate that he or she votes for.

Step 3 The assumptions are: (a) there is an equal number of Democrats and Republicans; (b) 75 percent of Democrats vote for the candidate of their party, and 80 percent of Republicans vote for the candidate of their party.

Step 4 We will model the simulation using a random number table and selecting *two* numbers. The first number (a one-digit number) will indicate the voter's choice. We will let D denote that the voter or the vote is Democratic, and R denote that the voter or the vote is Republican.

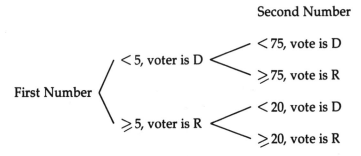

Step 5 Our trial consists of selecting the two random numbers. Our first trial resulted in RR, namely, a Republican voting Republican.

Step 6   The observation of interest is the outcome of the trial, namely:

DD: Democrat voting for a Democrat
DR: Democrat voting for a Republican
RD: Republican voting for a Democrat
RR: Republican voting for a Republican

Step 7   Repeat the trial. The outcomes of 100 trials are shown below.

RR	RR	DR	RR	DD	RD	RR	DD	DD	RD	DR	RR	RD
RR	RD	DD	DD	RD	DD	RR	RR	DD	DD	RR	DD	RR
RR	DD	DD	DR	DD	DD	DD	DD	DD	RR	RR	RR	DD
RR	RD	DD	RR	RR	RR	RR	DR	RR	DD	DD	DR	DD
RR	DD	RR	RR	RR	DD	DD	RD	DD	DD	DD	RR	DD
DR	DD	RR	RR	DR	DD	DD	DD	DD	RD	RR	DD	DR
DD	RR	DD	DD	RR	RR	DD	RR	RR	DD	RD	DD	DD
DD	DD	DD	RR	RR	DR	DD	RR	RD				

Step 8   Summarize the information. In this example, we can first count the number of trials with the different outcomes and then set up a table giving the counts for each outcome.

	Voting for Democrat	Voting for Republican
Democrat	45	9
Republican	10	36

This table can help us answer several questions. For example, what is the chance of a randomly selected voter being a Republican who would vote for a Democrat? The answer, based on the table, is $\frac{10}{100}$ or 0.1. Candidates running for office often use simulations like this one to help them in planning their campaign.

Application 19

Inherited Traits

The inheritance of physical traits is determined by the interaction of the parents' genes during reproduction. For example, the reason why you have blue or brown eyes is because of the genes you inherited from each of your parents. The same is true about the color of your skin or hair. One of the first scientists to discover the laws of heredity was Mendel. In his experiment, Mendel crossed two varieties of peas and found that the offspring of the crossed varieties showed the characteristics of the two original peas according to certain rules. We are going to find out the rule in this simulation.

Suppose you have a plant with red flowers and a plant with blue flowers, and you cross the two plants. The genes that determine the color for the flowers consist of two chromosomes, each of which carries either red (R) or blue (B) code. For the red flower, both chromosomes will be R, so the gene for the red flower can be shown as RR. Similarly, the gene for the blue flower will be BB. The plant we get by crossing red and blue flowering plants will inherit one chromosome from each plant. So we get a plant with purple flowers from crossing a red flowering plant and a blue flowering plant.

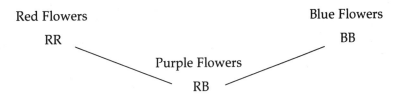

What would happen if we crossed two plants with purple flowers? This second-generation cross would also have genes represented by two letters, R and B, in different combinations.

The crossing of two purple flowering plants can be simulated by using two coins. Coin 1 represents one purple plant and coin 2 the second. For each coin, let heads denote the R chromosome and tails the B. Each coin is tossed once to simulate the generation of a particular offspring. If coin 1 comes up heads and coin 2 tails, then the offspring is RB, or another purple flower. Use this simulation model to answer the following questions.

1. What would be the possible colors of the flowers of the second generation of plants when the first-generation plants both have purple flowers?

2. Which color would occur most often? How frequently should it occur?

3. Can you suggest how you could simulate possible colors of flowers of the third generation? Remember, the colors for the offspring depend on the genes of the parents.

Turning Left

I can make a left turn onto a highway immediately after stopping if there is no car coming in either direction. The probability that a car is coming from the left is two thirds, and the probability that one is coming from the right is one half.

1. Estimate the probability that I can make a left turn without delay.

2. Find the theoretical probability that a car is *not* coming from the left and a car is *not* coming from the right. Compare your answer with the estimate obtained in question 1. What assumption did you make in this calculation?

3. How would you simulate the probability of making a left turn without delay two times in succession when traveling through this intersection?

Application 21

Power Systems

A primary power system, S_1, on a space shuttle has a backup system, S_2. If S_1 fails during a mission, S_2 automatically takes over. Suppose the probability that S_1 fails during a mission is 0.2, and the probability that S_2 fails is 0.3. Simulate the operation of these systems to answer the following questions.

1. What is the probability that at least one of the two power systems is operating at the end of the mission?

2. What is the probability that S_2 must be used on a mission?

3. What assumptions were made for your simulation? Do they seem reasonable?

(*Hint:* The operation of S_1 can be simulated by selecting a random digit from Table 6 (page 19) and letting 0 and 1 represent failure of the system. If the first number selected is a 0 or 1, S_1 fails, and a second number is selected to represent the operation of S_2; 0, 1, and 2 could represent failure of S_2. Thus, a first digit of 1 and a second digit of 5 would simulate the situation in which S_1 fails and S_2 does not fail.)

Shooting Foul Shots

   A basketball player shoots foul shots with a two-thirds accuracy record. That is, she has scored a basket on two out of every three attempts. She is given a free throw from the foul line and is given a second shot only if she has scored a basket on the first shot. In this one-and-one situation, she can score 0, 1, or 2 points. Design a simulation for this player's score on a trip to the free-throw line and use the simulation for 50 trials to answer the following questions.

1.   What is the average number of points per trip to the free-throw line?

2.   What number of points occurs most frequently?

3.   For what fraction of the trips to the free-throw line did the player shoot twice?

VI. SUPPLEMENTARY APPLICATIONS

Application 23

Chances of Meeting

Jon and Andrea want to meet at the library. Each agrees to arrive there between 1:00 and 1:30 P.M. They also agree to wait five minutes after arriving (but not after 1:30). If the other does not arrive during that five minutes, the first person will leave. What is the probability that Jon and Andrea will meet?

(*Hint:* Random times between 0 and 30 minutes can be selected from a random number table. Select two-digit numbers and eliminate those larger than 30.)

Making a Sale

The manager of a store that sells only TV sets has carefully observed her customers and sales for a long period of time. For a certain hour of the day, the probability is 0.3 that the store will have no customers, 0.6 that it will have one customer, and 0.1 that it will have two customers. Each customer has a probability of 0.2 of buying a TV set while in the store.

1. Estimate the probability that the manager will make at least one sale during this hour tomorrow.

2. Estimate the probability that the manager will make two sales during this hour.

3. What is this manager's average number of sales for this hour?

(*Hint:* Two random devices are needed, one to generate the number of customers and one to generate sales per customer. If the first device shows "no customers," then the second need not be used. If the first shows "one customer," the second must be used once to determine "sale" or "no sale." If the first shows "two customers," the second must be used twice.)

Application 25

Back and Forth

Let an x axis represent the path between a child's playground ($x = 0$) and her home ($x = 10$). Suppose we meet the child at $x = 5$. The child moves forward (from x to $x + 1$) and back (x to $x - 1$) with equal probability each minute. Design a simulation, and run it to estimate the mean number of minutes that it takes the child to reach either the playground or her home.

1. What is the average number of minutes it takes the child to reach either the playground or home?

2. For what fraction of the trials did the child reach home?

A Change in the Weather

Observations over a period of years gave the following information for July.

If today is sunny, then P(tomorrow is sunny) = 0.7
and P(tomorrow is dull) = 0.3

If today is dull, then P(tomorrow is sunny) = 0.5
and P(tomorrow is dull) = 0.5

Assuming that the first day of the month is sunny, design a simulation to find the mean number of consecutive sunny days in the first week in July.

1. What is the mean number of consecutive sunny days for that week?

2. What is the longest period of sunny days in your simulation?

3. If we assume instead that the first day is dull, do you think that the answers for questions 1 and 2 would change? Verify your answer with a simulation.

Application 27

Selling the News

The operator of a newsstand buys daily newspapers for 15 cents each and sells them for 25 cents each. His daily records show that the probability of selling exactly 20 newspapers is 0.2, and the probability of selling exactly 40 newspapers is 0.3. A newspaper left over at the end of the day represents a total loss, and a newspaper sold yields a profit of 10 cents. Design a simulation to study the number of customers per day—20, 30, or 40—with the given probabilities (use 50 trials).

1. Estimate the average number of customers per day.

2. Using the answer from question 1, estimate the operator's average profit if he buys 20, 30, or 40 newspapers. How many newspapers should the operator buy each day to maximize his profit, given that he can buy newspapers only in multiples of 10?

Unloading Trucks

A pea cannery is to be built in your town. Trucks will arrive randomly, with one arrival every four minutes on the average. Each truck can be unloaded in four minutes, once the cannery crew gets to the truck. Follow the steps below to determine whether this is a good arrangement for the cannery.

A. Use a shuffled deck of 52 cards.

B. Set a 20-minute work period. Each card turned represents one minute.

C. A diamond represents a truck arriving.

D. Keep track of:
1. What time each truck arrives.
2. What time each truck is unloaded.
3. The delay time for each truck driver.

E. Make a summary showing:
1. The number of trucks arriving per 20-minute period.
2. The amount of overtime (time worked by cannery workers beyond the 20-minute period).
3. The total delay time for each truck driver.

Following is an actual experiment, as an example.

Time (minute) Truck Arrived	Time (minute) Truck Unloaded	Delay (minutes)
1	5	0
5	9	0
11	15	0
16	20	0
17	24	3

Number of trucks arriving: 5
Overtime: 4 minutes
Delay time: 3 minutes

Perform the experiment 50 times. Does the situation appear to be good? If not, what changes would you make in the proposed cannery?

Application 29

The Soft-Drink Machine

A soft-drink machine that fills paper cups is set to dispense eight ounces of liquid each time it is operated. However, the actual amount of liquid dispensed will vary, sometimes being slightly over eight ounces and sometimes slightly under. If the machine is operating correctly, the *median* amount of liquid dispensed should be eight ounces.

One way to keep track of the operating characteristics of the machine is to record whether the amount dispensed is above or below the median for a series of fills. For example, a series of ten observations could result in LHLLLHHHHL or LLLHHHHHLL, with L denoting a low observation (below the median) and H denoting a high observation (above the median).

One way to look for a pattern in such data is to observe the number of *runs*, or sequences of like symbols. Series (a) results in 5 runs (3 L runs and 2 H runs), whereas series (b) results in 3 runs (2 L runs and 1 H run). For each series of ten observations, the number of runs could be any integer from 1 to 10. (All the runs could be H or L, or the runs of H's and L's could alternate.)

How can these data lead to decisions about how well the machine is functioning? If the number of runs is small (say, 1 or 2), we might think that something is causing the machine to give too many overfills or underfills. If the number of runs is fairly large, the machine is varying more often from high to low, which might be expected under normal operations. Thus, we might decide to adjust the machine if a *low* number of runs is observed.

We can simulate the behavior of ten observations from this machine by tossing a coin ten times. Let heads denote high (H) and tails denote low (L). If the machine is operating correctly, H and L are equally likely for any one observation. For the ten tosses, the number of runs should be recorded. This corresponds to one trial of ten observations. The simulation should then be repeated for at least 50 trials.

From your simulation results (which can be done by pooling information from groups of students), estimate the probabilities for the various numbers of runs as indicated below:

Number of Runs (in 10 measurements)	Estimated Probability
0	
1	
2	
3	
4	
5	
6	
7	
8	
9	
10	

1. What number of runs has the highest estimated probability?

2. What is the probability that the number of runs is three or fewer?

3. For what numbers of runs would you begin to suspect that the machine may not be functioning properly? Why?

Application 30

An Epidemic

The speed of an infectious disease can be modeled as follows. Suppose that an infectious disease has a one-day infection period, and after that a person is immune. Six people live on an otherwise deserted island. One person catches the disease and randomly visits one other person for help during the infection period. The second person is infected and visits another person at random during the next day (his infection period). The process continues, with one visit per day, until an infectious person visits an immune person and the disease dies out.

This simplified epidemic can be simulated by tossing a die. Suppose that the people, numbered 1 through 6, correspond to the die faces. Person 1 has the disease today. Roll the die to see whom he visits. (If you roll a 1, ignore it and roll again. A person cannot visit himself.) Then, roll again to see whom the second person visits. The die roll is repeated until an infectious person visits an immune person (one who has already had the disease). Construct at least 20 trials of the simulated epidemic. Use the simulation results to answer the following questions.

1. What is the average number of people who get the disease in your simulated epidemic?

2. What is the probability that more than three people get the disease?

3. What is the probability that all six people get the disease?